Space Explorer

THE MOON

Patricia Whitehouse

Heinemann Library
Chicago, Illinois

Customer Service 888-454-2279

Visit our website at www.heinemannlibrary.com

Designed by Heinemann Library
Printed in China by South China Printing.

08 07 06 05 04
10 9 8 7 6 5 4 3 2 1

Library of Congress Cataloging-in-Publication Data
Whitehouse, Patricia, 1958-
  Moon / Patricia Whitehouse.
     v. cm. -- (Space explorer)
  Includes bibliographical references and index.
  Contents: What is the moon? -- How big and how far away? -- A rocky surface -- Craters -- Seas, valleys, and mountains -- Black sky -- Hot and cold -- Gravity -- Moonlight -- Changing shape -- Phases of the moon -- Day and night moon -- Tides.
  ISBN 1-4034-5152-4 (lib. bdg.) -- ISBN 1-4034-5656-9 (pbk.)
  1. Moon--Juvenile literature. [1. Moon.] I. Title. II. Series.
  QB582.W48 2004
  523.3--dc22

                            2003026763

Acknowledgments
The author and publishers are grateful to the following for permission to reproduce copyright material:

Cover photograph: C.S. Neilsen/Bruce Coleman

p. 5 Getty Images/Photodisc; p. 7 Corbis (royalty free); p. 8 NASA; p. 9 Getty Images/Photodisc; p. 10 Getty Images/Photodisc; p. 11 NASA; p. 12 NASA; p. 13 NASA; p. 14 NASA; p. 15 Corbis (royalty free); p. 16 NASA/Science Photo Library; p. 17 NASA; p. 18 Corbis (royalty free); p. 19 NASA; p. 20 Corbis (royalty free); p. 22 David Nunuk/Science Photo Library; p. 24, Eckhard Slawick/Science Photo Library; p. 25 Eckhard Slawick/Science Photo Library; p. 26 Getty Images/Photodisc; p. 27 NASA; p. 28 David Thompson/Oxford Scientific Films; p. 29 David Thompson/Oxford Scientific Films

Every effort has been made to contact copyright holders of any material reproduced in this book. Any omissions will be rectified in subsequent printings if notice is given to the publisher.

Special thanks to Geza Gyuk of the Adler Planetarium for his comments in preparation of this book.

Some words are shown in bold, **like this.** You can find out what they mean by looking in the glossary.

Contents

What Is the Moon?

The Moon is a huge ball of rock and metal that **orbits** Earth. It is Earth's **satellite.** A satellite is something that orbits a planet.

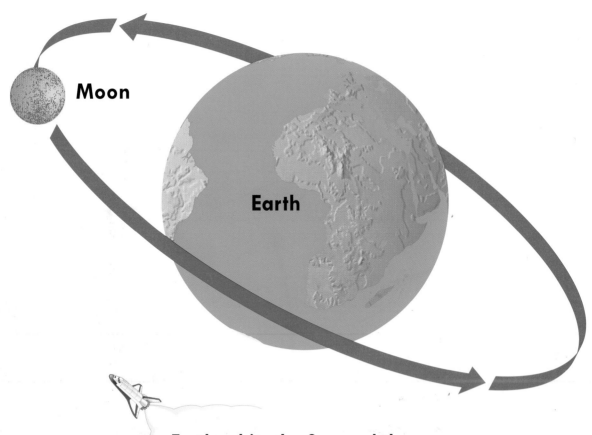

Moon

Earth

Earth orbits the Sun and the Moon orbits Earth.

One side of the
Moon always faces
Earth. The other side
always faces away.
People on Earth can
see only one side of
the Moon.

The Moon is 2,160 miles (3,476 kilometers) across. This is about four times smaller than Earth. About 50 moons could fit inside Earth.

Earth

7,927 miles
(12,756 kilometers)

Moon

2,160 miles
(3,476 kilometers)

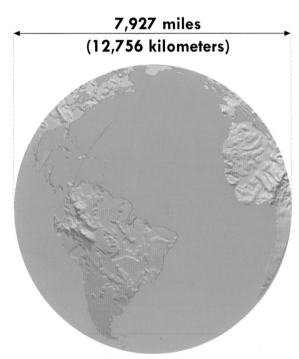

Earth is about four times wider than the Moon.

If you hold your arm out straight, you can block your view of the Moon with your thumb. The Moon looks small because it is 238,860 miles (384,390 kilometers) away.

A Rocky Surface

The Moon is made up of rocks, metals, and dust. There is no water on the Moon. Scientists think a small amount of ice might be buried beneath the Moon's **surface** near its north pole.

Astronauts brought back samples of different Moon rocks for scientists to study.

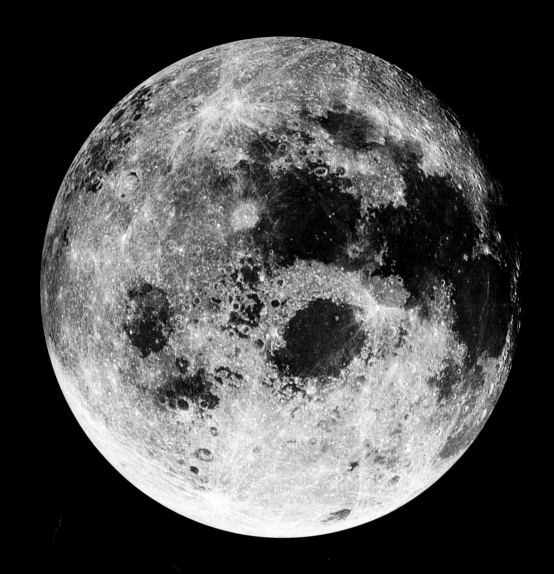

The dust on the Moon was made when **meteorites** crashed into it and broke rocks apart. The dark and light areas we can see show that the Moon is made of different kinds of rocks.

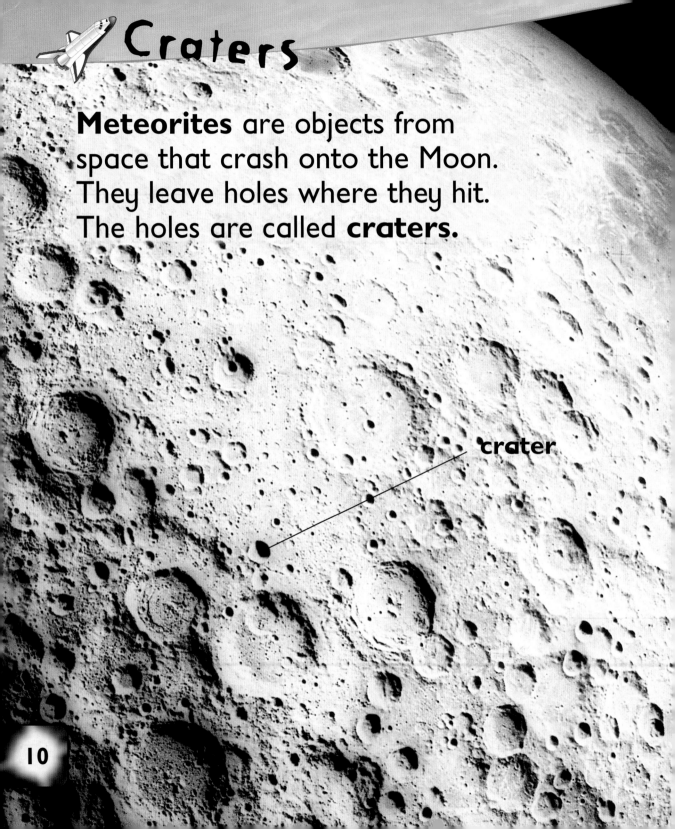

Craters

Meteorites are objects from space that crash onto the Moon. They leave holes where they hit. The holes are called craters.

crater

Aitken Basin

Craters can be the size of your
fingernail or several hundred miles or
kilometers in size. The largest crater
is called The Aitken Basin. It is 1,398
miles (2,250 kilometers) across.

Seas and Mountains

Long ago, people thought the dark parts of the Moon were seas of water. Now we know they were once **lava** flows. The dark patches are still called seas.

Sea of Serenity

Sea of Showers

Sea of Tranquility

Ocean of Storms

Sea of Fertility

Like the Earth, the Moon has valleys and mountains. The tallest Moon mountains are the Apennines, which are about 19,685 feet (6,000 meters) high.

The large mountain behind the astronaut is called Hadley Rille. The mountain to the left of it is Hadley Delta.

The Earth is covered by a layer of **gas** called the **atmosphere.** The Sun shining through this makes the sky look blue. The Moon does not have an atmosphere, so the sky always looks black.

This astronaut's footprint has not
changed in over 35 years.

There is no weather on the Moon.
This means that wind and rain do
not change **craters** and other Moon
features. They can stay the same for
millions of years.

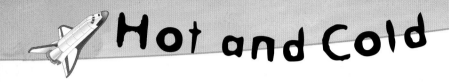

The Moon is either very hot or very cold. The Sun's heat causes the Moon to reach 266 °F (130 °C). That is the **temperature** of a warm oven on Earth.

This is what the Sun looks like from the Moon.

16

Temperatures are very cold at night and in the shadows of the mountains. Temperatures can reach −290 °F (−179 °C). That is colder than any place on Earth.

This is what the dark side of the Moon looks like.

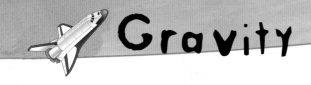

Gravity is the force that pulls everything toward the center of the Earth. It is why people and animals on Earth do not float away from the Earth's **surface.**

It takes a lot of energy to jump this high on Earth.

Earth's gravity is about six times stronger than the Moon's gravity. On the Moon, you could jump six times higher than you can on Earth.

Even with heavy space suits, astronauts move around easily in the Moon's low gravity.

19

Moonlight

The Moon is the brightest object in our sky at night. But the Moon does not make its own light.

The Moon is lit up by the Sun.

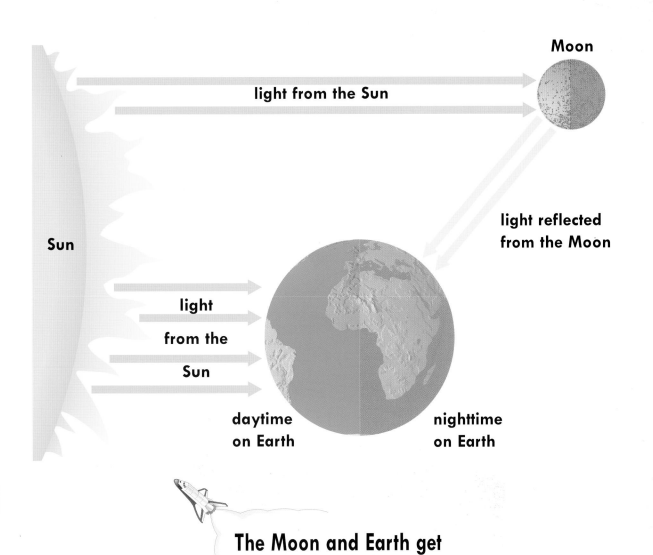

Moon

light from the Sun

Sun

light reflected from the Moon

light

from the

Sun

daytime on Earth

nighttime on Earth

The Moon and Earth get light from the Sun.

Moonlight is really sunlight! The light from the Sun travels to the Moon. The sunlight bounces off the Moon's **surface** and travels to Earth.

Changing Shape

The Moon seems to change shape. It goes from a round shape to a thin crescent, then back again. It takes 29 $\frac{1}{2}$ days to do this. This time is called a lunar month.

When the Moon looks thin, it is because we can only see a bit of the side that is lit up.

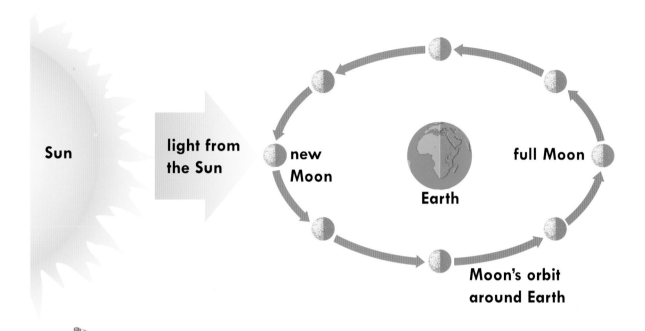

Sun

light from
the Sun

new
Moon

Earth

full Moon

Moon's orbit
around Earth

The Moon moves around Earth, and each
night we see a different amount of the side
that has sunlight on it.

The Moon's **orbit** around Earth
changes how much of the Moon we
see. The shape of the Moon in our
sky depends on how much sunlight
is bounced toward Earth.

Phases of the Moon

The changing shapes of the Moon are called **phases.** The **full Moon** phase is a circle shape. Then the Moon gets smaller.

new Moon

full Moon

When the Moon is between the Sun and Earth, we cannot see any reflected sunlight. The Moon cannot be seen. This is the **new Moon** phase.

new
Moon

Day and Night

The Moon is not just out at night.
It is often out during the day.
We can sometimes see it
in the morning or in
the late afternoon.

The Moon coming up is called moonrise. The Moon going down is called moonset. Sometimes the Moon looks larger and orange at moonrise.

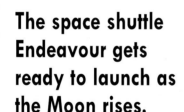

The space shuttle Endeavour gets ready to launch as the Moon rises.

27

Tides

The Moon's **gravity** pulls on Earth's oceans. This causes the water level on shore to change. These changes of water levels are called tides.

At low tide, the Moon pulls the water away from the shore, so more of the shore shows. At high tide, the water moves back onto the shore.

Amazing Moon Facts

- People see shapes in the patterns of light and dark patches on the Moon. Some people think it looks like a human's face.

- Twelve astronauts have landed on the Moon.

- Astronauts brought 842 pounds (382 kilograms) of Moon rocks back to Earth.

- The Moon's craters have names. Many of the craters are named after famous scientists.

Glossary

atmosphere thick layer of gases around a planet

crater hole caused by a meteorite hitting the surface of a planet, moon, or other object

full Moon phase of the Moon that is a circle shape

gas airlike material that is not solid or liquid

gravity force that pulls objects together

lava melted rock

meteorite an object from space, made of stone or metal, that crashes onto a planet or moon

new Moon phase of the Moon in which the Moon cannot be seen

orbit the path one object takes around another

phase one part of a cycle

reflect bounce off

satellite object that orbits a planet or a moon

surface top or outside of an object

More Books to Read

Ganeri, Anita. *Day and Night (Nature's Patterns)*. Chicago: Heinemann Library, 2004.

Whitehouse, Patricia. *The Earth (Space Explorer)*. Chicago: Heinemann Library, 2004.

Index